# Ins and Outs
# of Heaven

**A True Story:
Jenna's Visits to
and from Heaven**

**Our True 'Cycle of Life' Unveiled**

# Jenna Orion

Some of the names of the people in this true story have been changed to protect their privacy.

Library of Congress Cataloging-in-Publication Data
Orion, Jenna

Ins And Outs of Heaven
Orion, Jenna

www.InsAndOutsOfHeaven.com

Published by Universal Changes, Inc.
Printed in the United States of America

ISBN-10: 0692520678
ISBN-13: 978-0692520673

# CONTENTS

# ACKNOWLEDMENTS

Thanks to my spiritual guides, companions and protectors of humanity who are much like Jesus; they are highly evolved, spiritually enlightened all-knowing entities that I collectively call my guides and teachers. Without them, I would not have the ins and outs of Heaven to share with you. I also wish to thank them for their continual, diligent work to protect humanity, and improve our quality of life and beyond with their teachings.

I would like to give a special thank you to my daughter for being my best friend throughout life. I also would like to thank my multi-talented granddaughters for their love and support.

I want to acknowledge and give thanks to those who have passed on for their contribution to my life and this book, both before and after their deaths, especially to my mother and father. In life, my father worked endlessly to provide a great life for his family. My mother was the best mother in the world; her entire life was spent in service to her family and God. In the afterlife both of my parents have continued to be in touch to support me with their new found knowledge in Heaven.

Thanks to my longtime friends Sue, Pam, and Paul, who have given me moral support to keep sharing the knowledge I receive. In addition I want to give a special thank you to my friends Di and Daniel for all of their assistance and interest in my work. I appreciate their willingness to lend a hand when needed. Last but not least, thanks to my longtime friend Laurie Hannan Anton, an entertainment attorney, who has been available to assist me.

'Ins and outs of Heaven' is the true story of my journey through life to discover a roadmap to Heaven through star-gazing. I had the same unanswered questions that most of us have; how does the cycle of life truly function, is Heaven real, where is it, how do we get there, and will I see my loved ones again who have passed on?

I sought those answers and more from a place out in the Heavens where all-encompassing God-like love, peace, and harmony exist.

As a result of my curiosity I have lived a very fascinating life; I gained answers to our unanswered questions as magical manifestations began to appear out of thin air and events were orchestrated in my life to bring those answers. I later learned that all of these events were created for me by a group of highly evolved , spiritually enlightened Master type entities that I collectively call my guides; they are much like Jesus in their evolutionary status.

I ultimately received a visit at my home from one of these guides. He lifted the veil to allow me to watch our 'full cycle of life in action'; on that day I witnessed a 'forever life' that has no end. As it turns out the details of this entire experience are very complex, nevertheless they are outlined in detail in this book.

Throughout my life I have experienced many trips to Heaven, as well as receiving visitors from Heaven; each visit contributing facts that validate that Heaven is a real physical place.

Those same guides provided the answers to our heartfelt questions through a 'roadmap to Heaven 9.0!'

Compiled as one seamless story of facts, magical manifestations and unique experiences, I am now able to share the answers with you that I have spent many years star-gazing to unveil. Here's hoping that this big picture will make living life more user friendly for all of us, especially for those with failing health.

You mentally asked some of the same questions as I did; voila, the answers to your questions are now at your fingertips.

## DEDICATION TO HUMANITY

This educational book was created for the purpose of allowing humanity to get back to living life in the manner in which it was originally intended. Life can be more user-friendly and stress free when our true cycle of life and our evolutionary process is fully understood.

The nature of reality has been distorted over the years, causing major confusion in modern society. This in turn has caused many to stray off their intended path and purpose for living.

The collective energy of society and Earth can move into a more positive direction with the simple understanding of life's process as it was unveiled to me.

"If you want to find the secret of the universe, think in terms of energy, frequency and vibration."

NikolaTesla

"My brain is only a receiver, in the universe there is a core from which we obtain knowledge, strength and inspiration. I have not penetrated into the secrets of this core, but I know that it is exists."

Nikola Tesla

## Topic # 1:  Early Spiritual Teachings

As a child I went to either a Christian or a Methodist church almost every Sunday.  I had a Sunday school teacher to educate me about God and how life's process works.  Those teachings didn't always add up for me; there were always missing pieces.  When I asked for answers to the missing pieces I was often told, "Those are things we are not supposed to know." That didn't make any sense to me either, as I thought there was an answer to everything.  Their teachings were for the purpose of giving me faith in God but what they gave me was confusion and a lot of unanswered questions.  I am a very detail oriented person, so I need all of the facts in order to get the big picture, not just a portion of them.

As I looked back on my journey through life I flashed back to my childhood days when my favorite thing to do was lie in the grass and look up at the night sky.  I felt a connection 'out there' and a sense of peace and calm when gazing at the stars.

My method of getting answers to those unanswered questions was to mentally search for them as I gazed at the sky.  I felt as though the answers were out there and that someday I would get all of them; I was on a mission as I continued my star-gazing.

Since I hadn't bought into the explanations I was given about how life works from the dogmatic, religious viewpoint, I just tried to stay tuned in to nature and stay connected to my spirit or soul as much as I did my physical body. I allowed the connection I felt with the stars to stay present with me.

When going to bed after a night of gazing at the stars, I felt as though I was not alone. I could sense something around my solar plexus area that felt harmonious and safe. It was as if someone like a guardian Angel was watching over me, which made no sense to me at that time.

At that point, I decided that instead of accepting the answers, or lack thereof, from the religious teachers, I would no longer consider myself to be religious; I would just be spiritual. With that philosophy I stayed open minded and allowed my soul to teach me whatever it had to offer.  This new way of thinking took me on a journey of many twists and turns while searching for the answers to those same unanswered questions that many of us have.  When the answers did come to me, they came in unusual ways. They always made sense and seemed very natural.

In the end, I found the missing pieces to the puzzle of life and understood how the cycle of life really works; in essence, I was presented a roadmap to Heaven. I had no idea that one day I would take many trips out there into the universe where I would often end up in Heaven and still be able to return to Earth. I didn't realize that I would one day have visitors from Heaven coming to me right here on Earth to communicate, but that is exactly what happened. I had no idea why I felt connected to something out there in that vast sky; I just felt it was normal to connect with whatever it was and it helped me stay emotionally balanced.

## Topic # 2:  Spiritual Guidance

My life has been like a treasure hunt to find Heaven and to find out what our connection to God is; it paid off because I found both and much more.

I discovered that I have several of these highly evolved spiritual Master type guides that watch over me; each one of them exudes a different spiritual energy that has its own identity. I have learned to discern who each one is by their spirit/aura that exudes the loving essence of who they really are; each Master's distinctive energy acts as their identifier instead of a face.

I have always known Jesus as a person and I viewed him as a friend in just the same manner as I knew anyone on Earth. This is not to say that He was on the same spiritual level as people on Earth but in reality He is someone I have known in the past.

Many people use different terminology to describe their experiences with a source that is more highly evolved than we are. Some have stated that Jesus answers their prayers by doing things for them or giving them something, just as I was taught in my childhood. Instead of using the word prayer, I call it meditation; it is the same thing except that in my meditation, I don't ask God to do something for me, I ask what I can do for the higher good of humanity, to fulfill my purpose here on Earth and to know what I need to know.

Some people state that God is speaking to them. Some say it is an Angel or an Ascended Master who spoke to them, some even use the term 'God Source' instead of God. Each person defines this type of communication differently. In essence, what they and their soul know is that they are being communicated with by an entity that is of a higher spiritual wisdom than we are.

The Master type entities that I collectively call my guides speak to me telepathically, use thought transfer, and create events in my life.  They have an uncanny way of doing this. Every time it seems as though the event was just a coincidence, later I find that the event had been orchestrated by my guides to give me clarity on a particular new teaching.

I have had a long lifetime of visits with these various Masters with great powers.  I recall a time when I was traveling for work and staying at a hotel.  At that time I felt as though I was stuck in a

3

work place that wasn't flowing with the universe or my life's mission, so I decided to seek assistance through meditation.

I was centering myself and getting into my higher consciousness, when suddenly, I felt a very powerful presence in the room. I had just started to pray to Jesus for guidance on the next step in my life's mission. Suddenly my hair follicles were standing on end from a God-like energy that I felt right in front of me. I sensed the outline of this male figure as if I was looking at a solid person.

Since I was praying to Jesus, I assumed it was Him. This male Entity then started to communicate with me. I immediately interrupted His speech and asked, "Are you Jesus?" He replied through a loud and clear telepathic communication: "No, I am referred to as 'Ancient of Days' in the Bible. I have come to tell you to leave your current work and proceed with your own spiritual service as our spokesperson for a higher teaching. You have much work to do to help the people of your planet."

I communicate with these entities, my guides, in the same manner that others communicate with God or Jesus and I feel protected by them. I know I am also protected by my soul and gut feelings as well; it is the powerful force that we each possess and the guidance we are meant to live by. This soul guidance allows me to end up in the right place at just the right time without effort when I pay attention to its promptings; it is normal and effortless. I have to listen and heed the soul guidance for it to be successful.

The spiritually enlightened beings are assisting me with specific things because they want those things shared with the public. As I said earlier, they consider me as their spokesperson. Their multi-faceted teachings allow us to know who we really are, what the true nature of reality is, where we came from, where we go when we leave Earth, as well as how we get to Heaven. They have shared with me the details of how the universe, and our cycle of life truly functions.

When they communicate with me, they use two methods: telepathic dictations and a form of communication known as 'thought transfer.' It is merely a mental transfer of words of knowledge from a guide with a higher spiritual consciousness than mine. The spiritual guide merges consciousness with me and transfers a series of words to my soul and it is then received by the brain.

The first time this happened to me, it started out as a sentence that was telepathically being transmitted to me, then in the middle of the sentence the words changed course and were transmitted through the soul and ended up becoming my thoughts. At that point, I could verbally voice this information to the listener as if they are my words or thoughts; it is all happening almost simultaneously, although I am aware at that time that those words were transferred to me and were not really my thoughts. I believe they did it this way so that I would be aware of how the transfer takes place. I look forward to a day when they do more of this type of communication due to the convenience of receiving knowledge so directly.

This process is totally different than a trance channeling situation where an entity takes over your physical body; **that never happens to me** because I clearly stated in the beginning of my work with the guides that I would never want to be a trance channeler. They have honored this request since they are all about allowing free will.

They never control me; my soul's higher consciousness is what controls me while working in unison with my physical body. These guides are of the highest spiritual realm and would not be allowed to control anyone, as that would be against the natural laws of the universe. They respect and follow those laws because the entire universe works in unison with Earth and the various dimensions that exist.

### Topic # 3: Forever Already Is

As I moved on with my mission, my guidance continued to assist me. One morning I awoke to an intense spiritual energy in the room. I could feel it penetrating every cell of my soul and body. I quickly discovered that I had a visitor. He was not from Heaven; he was from a dimension that is of a higher plane of existence than Heaven is. He possesses pure love and perfect balance. He is a spiritually enlightened Ascended Master type guide that I felt as if I had known prior to this lifetime.

Meeting with Him, Jesus, or any of my other guides feels like meeting someone close to God. I feel an overpowering, natural God-like love energy that emanates from them; it is a feeling that is difficult to fully describe. Their energy is so powerful it penetrated every cell of my body during our meetings; it is like becoming a part of them. A small amount of that God-like energy stays with me when they leave. I gradually get used to it being there and then it seems to slowly fade away or at least it becomes less noticeable; it feels perfectly normal for this process to occur.

This particular entity, like my other guides, is easily identifiable by His soul's energy. I consider this entity to be one of my guides because He had assisted me many times since the day I was born. On this visit I had a powerful experience with Him that started me on the road to finding the answers to some of the age old questions that I had as a star-gazing child: questions about God, the universe, and how our lives evolve.

At this particular visit, the veil was totally lifted for me for a short while for the purpose of granting me the ability to see into our 'forever life,' a life that never ends. I looked into forever and I saw 'all that is': everything that is, ever was, and ever will be, happening all at once. I realized that this is the true nature of reality. I like to call it the 'isness principle'—it just is. It is where all knowledge that already exists can be found. There, I witnessed our 'cycle of life in action,' the entirety of how life's evolutionary cycle and basic structure functions.

It all felt so natural and obvious at the time, but it is pretty mind-boggling to think about now.

Part of what I saw was the process of getting to Heaven, as well as our ability to travel back and forth to Heaven while still in an earthly physical body.  There are many pieces to this true reality and I will address each one as we go along.

What I saw that morning was so complex that it took me years to sort it all out and be able to suitably describe it.  Some of those things I witnessed that day do not exactly match up with what I was taught in church regarding God and how life's cycle functions. I think this particular experience was one of the first times I realized that what we think of as reality is not reality at all.  I, as well as many others, have been living someone else's explanation of truth.

It was such a cool experience to see what I was privileged to. I knew that I would be given more details about this new reality in the future. After that event, I had many experiences that proved to me that what I witnessed when looking into 'All That Is' is in fact the way life's journey truly has happened long before we came to Earth and the way it will continue long after we leave Earth this time.

'All that is' is the core of all the teachings that I receive. It was the catalyst that enabled me to share this information with you. I consider it a privilege to have been shown this knowledge and I am grateful for what I have witnessed.

I am grateful that I can share these teachings to improve life's journey for those who are open-minded enough to accept them, and to give confirmation to those who already possess this same knowledge.

## Topic # 4: A Secretive Life

My unique experiences have always been a normal way of life for me. I never had a reason to question them until a friend who had witnessed some of these so-called unusual events play out in my life told me that not everyone has these kinds of experiences, not even her. After being told that I was different, I decided to keep my life private to avoid being criticized. I eventually had the nerve to speak out through the help of several great friends that I consulted with.

I am sure I am not the only one having this kind of experience. When I do meet someone with similar experiences, I find that most of them are not brave enough to tell their story. It took me years to get the nerve to tell mine, so I totally understand that most of society prefers to sweep their experiences under the rug if it doesn't fit in with the social consciousness.

During my experiences with life's spiritual evolutionary processes, there was a time when I was in confusion about the validity of my trips to Heaven or visitors coming to me from Heaven because according to my religious teachings this isn't supposed to happen. No matter how much I argued with myself about these visits, they continued to happen; consequently, I finally realized that the visits were real. Thank God, many others have now seen the light, literally, and are not afraid to speak about this subject in public.

With the discovery of how the cycle of life, our forever Life, really works I have gained the answers to the mysteries of the ages. I am happy to share this information, as I know this was the intended purpose for my receiving the information to begin with.

Throughout life, my experiences have been fascinating, miraculous, and positive. These positive but unique occurrences escalated in frequency as time went on; therefore, it left no doubt that these seemingly coincidental events were really no coincidence after all, but rather orchestrated and carried out by these highly evolved guides.

I decided to compile all the pieces of information that I had discovered; when completed, they painted a clear picture of a new reality for me and cleared my confusion. At that point, my compilation made more logical sense than what I had been taught in spiritual and religious settings in the past. I now know beyond a shadow of a doubt that Heaven is a real place in our universe.

## Topic # 5: Heaven's Location

Heaven is the mysterious place that everyone has heard about but most are not exactly sure where it's located, or how or when we will get there. Some wonder if we lay in a grave until Jesus comes back, what happens after we get to Heaven, will we be staying there forever, and is that all there is to life?

The answers to these questions are important for people to receive for several reasons.

After someone has lost a loved one due to death, it can destroy one's happiness. They don't know if they will ever see that person again; it can be very emotionally traumatizing and can cause a person to become physically ill.

This is probably one of the most important reasons why everyone should understand the true cycle of life to reduce the fear and anxiety that goes along with these situations.

I have seen stress relieved from many people after the one left behind is able to make some kind of contact with the deceased after they have left Earth. Just knowing for sure that they are in a better place and that there really is a Heaven where they can make contact and eventually reunite again is all very comforting.

Even though you will further develop spiritually when you are in Heaven; this doesn't mean you will not see others that are more or less evolved than you.

Heaven is just another location in the universe, another dimension of reality and plane of existence. It is the place where we go to after we leave Earth due to death. Heaven is different from Earth in many ways, although there are many mansions, cathedrals, and all types of buildings there that are similar to what we have here on Earth. Life goes on there in this beautiful place that has a euphoric God-like love energy and a sense of total peacefulness. The colors there are more alive than colors we have here on Earth; even though they are similar, there seems to be light within the colors that makes each one brighter and more vibrant.

After we pass on, our soul leaves the current physical body and takes on another physical body in Heaven; a new, more youthful and perfected body. I have witnessed this fact many times and one of the interesting things is that this new body looks the same but is always younger.

All in our life contributes to our evolutionary process. There are lessons to be learned in Heaven just as on Earth, but under more pleasant circumstances. It is a place where we study and learn just as we do on Earth until we reincarnate again to another planet or star for the purpose of fulfilling a mission. This new mission is assigned and selected because your help is or will be needed at some point. You may also have issues to work out at that location while in a physical body, such as karmic issues that need to be resolved.

While in this new incarnation back on Earth or in another dimension or planet, we also have the ability to continue to raise our spiritual awareness, which raises our soul level to a higher consciousness. When we leave this new incarnation due to death, we again go to a dimension that matches our current spiritual level so we can regroup and regenerate again.

After each lifetime we need to go back to heaven for several reasons. Going to Heaven is kind of like going to rehab for a reset; you become who you really are once again. When in Heaven we will be living more fully in the soul than in the physical, even though we take on a physical body and function there, the soul's consciousness is more in charge.

That's the good news, and the new information you receive in Heaven will always exist in your soul just as what you learned on Earth. The bad news is that when you go into your next incarnation you won't be able to recall all of that information immediately; however, the usual process of the soul guiding you each step of the way will take place. It will be revealed to you to the degree you allow it and when it is needed.

During my visits to Heaven, the major thing that really stood out to me was how different life functions there than on Earth. Like I mentioned before, the energy you feel there is so calm and peaceful compared to Earth. The feeling I got being with residents of Heaven felt as though they don't have a care in the world; they just go with the flow effortlessly. It is instant relief from life on Earth.

Heaven functions in perfection. During my visits to Heaven, I have never experienced anything that would indicate that they have any type of time-keeping system, such as we do with our clocks; nothing has ever been referred to regarding a time element. While visiting there I have always felt there was no need for such an instrument there. Everything there 'just is.'

The atmosphere is like everyone is living in the moment and everyone just lets things happen instead of trying to make them happen; it's as if they don't have a schedule or sense of time. I actually feel their system works seamlessly and everyone is in the right place at just the right time and it all gets done. I would love to live this system on Earth. I am sure we wouldn't need medical doctors if that were the case; Earth living is stressful for most people.

As I relived some of the experiences I had in Heaven, I realized how hectic life really is here on Earth. Everyone, including me, is off and running when they get out of bed. We all book way more than the average person could possibly get done. I am now realizing how this lifestyle creates enough stress to make us have health problems.

I am grateful to have had those pleasant experiences and to be able to tap into it again and relive the pleasant feeling that exists there. I try to incorporate that peaceful ambience into my daily life as much as possible.

## Topic # 6: This Exit: Heaven

Most of the things I learned in the experiences with my guides and the visits   to and from Heaven were never mentioned by our preachers and teachers in my early years. I now have enough of the missing pieces that I lacked in my early years to lead the way through life, into Heaven and beyond. Life's evolutionary cycle now makes logical sense after the new teachings and my Heavenly experiences. There is always more to know; therefore, I will stay open and learn because all of this is fascinating to me. I want to know more about various lifeforms out there in the universe and multiverses as well.

In order to travel to Heaven for visits all you need to know is that you have the ability to do so.  As time goes on, it will be easier for us to go back and forth to Heaven and go into the future due to the fact that I feel a higher spiritual energy that is steadily increasing on the Earth that will make this possible.

Our acquaintances that have passed into Heaven have the power to visit us for brief periods of time. They can't stay long in our environment and most likely wouldn't want to leave Heaven after being in such a peaceful place to come back to this chaos.

While living on Earth, most of us have patterned our life by the image that someone else has created for us through various religious and societal teachings. In essence, we are living someone else's truth.

Leaving the physical human body on Earth allows the veil to be more fully lifted so that you can see more of reality or what life is all about.  I am sure there are a lot of people that have had the veil fully lifted while living on Earth in a physical body; they are the ones that have dedicated their life to this purpose and live it daily.

I had some of these new teachings confirmed when my Mother paid a visit to me after she had passed on into Heaven. She wanted to point out during this visit that I should stay on the path I was on for spiritual evolution and that I was correct about the things I told her regarding the teachings I had received in the past. She learned this in hindsight while she was in Heaven, as she was also studying the same things there that I had studied here on Earth.

Before she died she thought I was too 'new age,' because she was taught in her youth to believe that you die, go into a grave and stay there until Jesus comes back to get you. Later in life, she had started to accept the fact that some of the things I believe were actually true when she saw the way I live my life: always being the best person I can be and always willing to help others to the extent of creating a lack for myself.

## Topic # 7: Magical Manifestations

Several of my friends and family members who are still on Earth have also had visits with their loved ones after their deaths. It seems that this is a pretty common event, though usually not discussed publicly. What is not common, however, is a female visitor appearing to me "out of the blue," literally. It takes a very powerful spiritual entity to create such an event.

At the time this event occurred, I was enjoying a beautiful day in sunny Florida. I am always excessively happy when I am near the beach. This day was no exception and to add to the joy I was feeling, I was about to experience a unique visitor in a manner that was truly out of the norm, even for me. I would call this miraculous. All I can say is that even I could not believe my eyes this time as this visitor made her way onto the scene in a big way.

This event happened after I had heard about a lady in Conyers, Georgia who was inviting the public to her location on Sundays to hear her 'Messages from Mother Mary.' She spoke about her visits with Mother Mary, who had appeared to her and was giving her messages for people on Earth. It was on the national television news the first time I heard about her experience.

After I heard about these public events, I was in a meditation and received a loud and clear message: "Please take your life story and our messages to the public in the same manner as the lady in Conyers, Georgia." I scratched my head, so to speak, thinking that I would not be brave enough to put myself out to the public and tell about the amazing things in my life. I would be concerned that the men in the white coats would be paying me a visit for the fitting of a straight-jacket. In fact, I sometimes feel as though they have been waiting in the wings for me to step out there so they can do just that.

On the day of this bizarre event I had gone down to the southeastern coast of Florida to visit a friend whose business is on the ocean. We had a long lunch at an ocean-side restaurant before I left to head back home. I felt a strong, positive energy in the air as I drove back north along the ocean road. It was very relaxing and peaceful as I drove in my customized van. With the large, front window on this type of vehicle, I had a great view of what was ahead of and above me.

As I drove along, out of the blue, I heard a telepathic voice say, "Look up." I immediately looked up at the sky and out over the ocean. My eyes were wide open, and they suddenly fixed on a sight. I was afraid to blink for fear of missing something. I was looking at an enlarged woman's face in the sky. My first thought was, "What on Earth?!" I blinked my eyes a few times and quickly wondered if an entire body was going to show up in mid-air in full body. And no, I wasn't drinking or on medication. This was quick, maybe a couple of minutes, but she was as real as anything I see on any normal day. This lady's head and face covered the entire sky in front of me!

Her face was very alive, and she was looking directly at me. Her expression was frozen when I first saw her, as if I was seeing a picture. Then I felt the mental connection to her presence and knew that she was acknowledging that I had seen her and mentally connected to her. Once she realized that I was connecting with her, she burst into a wide smile as our eyes met.

Her face was as clear as any photograph, yet it was alive; it was definitely as alive as you and me. The head and face were not a cloud in the shape of a head. It was a real face superimposed over the sky. What a shock!!!!

I know; I keep using the word alive to drive the point home, but she was so alive. How could that be possible? When I write about it, I can't help but express how shocking it was. Again, I could barely believe my own eyes, but that was exactly what happened. It certainly left nothing to the imagination. I know that it seems impossible for it to have happened, but it did!

I was really lucky that I didn't have a wreck. Time stood still for me. When the event was over and the face had disappeared, I found that I had slowed down but was still driving along the ocean-side road, despite the fact that my eyes were firmly fixed on her face in the sky until she vanished.

I could not give this female face a name because it was not a face that I recognized from appearance but I felt I knew her or had known her before. Her essence felt very God-like. I feel that 'She' is one of my Angelic spiritual protectors and had appeared in this manner as a means to motivate me to go public in the manner that the lady in Conyers, Georgia did. She was not someone from my family or friend who had passed into Heaven; she was like one of my extremely powerful guides.

I was not shown in any way shape or form what her name is; even though I think I know who it is, it is still a mystery as I have not had any confirmation of that. I would never say or write a statement like that unless I had received confirmation, as my work is always based on being one hundred percent honest. I have enough bizarre events that I don't have a reason to make something up or exaggerate it.

After receiving the guidance to go public just as the lady in Georgia did, I then realized why I had seen the face in the sky. Unfortunately, I was still not brave enough to honor that request at the time.

A whole new reality has been unveiled for me, a new reality that is a truth that resonates within my soul. It has given me a firm, spiritual foundation that has created a whole new meaning for life and taught me that anything is possible, especially after this event.

## Topic # 8:  The Evolutionary Cycle of the Soul

Our soul is who we really are. We are not the physical body in which the soul resides; the body is a temporary vehicle for the soul to use during each lifetime. The brain stores the information gained in your present lifetime but the soul records all that we do every instant. Everything about us, everything we have ever done, and everything we have ever learned is stored in our soul forever. This is what creates our spiritual evolution.

When we first receive information through hearing or viewing we get an instant gut feeling about that information. The soul is filtering the information for you before it gets to the brain. The soul is located in the solar plexus area; hence the term 'gut feeling.'

The soul has been and always will be the same original soul that we were at the beginning of time. The soul is neither male nor female. The original soul is one but it is branched out or split into more than one soul, which enables that same soul to be in more than one life at a time. That soul takes on a new physical body for each incarnation while still remaining the same soul. At the time the souls split off, each becomes a parallel soul to the others; so in essence, each one from the same group would be considered a parallel soul.  When they all reunite and become one, they will be complete.

The soul is our main guiding force. The gut feeling or the soul feeling is the first to warn us about the things that we need to know. The soul always recognizes the truth and can never be misled; it is your most important guide, one that will never fail to keep you protected if you pay attention. This process happens so quickly and is sometimes so subtle that we often feel or sense the warning but instantly forget it because we are moving on to the next thing so quickly. The brain is in control at that point and moves us right along; the brain loves to stay in control to keep you on the physical path throughout life.

At the time the thing we were warned about happens we instantly recall the warning. Don't you just hate it when that happens? I know I do; it happens to me all too frequently when I have not taken the time to balance my spiritual and physical life.

We need to stay tuned-in to our soul for guidance as our spiritual guides may not always be there when we want or need guidance; therefore we have to learn to think with our soul, our heart or our gut feeling instead of our brain or calling upon a guide in order to achieve what we need to do. If we live our life primarily for the physical and material aspect of it by using the brain more than the soul, we will not evolve as quickly as we would have if we had done the reverse.

Our soul is attached to our physical body by an invisible cord called the silver cord; it keeps the soul and body connected until death. It is much like the umbilical cord connecting mother and baby during pregnancy. This cord keeps our soul attached to our physical body so the soul can roam about the universe without the physical body; that process is called soul travel or astral travel and is very common. The silver cord automatically releases when the body is no longer functioning and you are ready to go to Heaven.

In order to more efficiently achieve what we set out to do in this life, it is helpful to learn to think with our soul, our heart or our gut feeling instead of our brain. This will give us a jump start and ignite our soul memory. When we learn to understand and think of our soul as who we really are instead of our physical body defining who we are, we are on the correct path to assist our soul in spiritually evolving in life's normal cycle.

The outward appearance of the physical body is what others normally recognize us by. You can also be recognized by the essence your soul or the energy of your soul emits. As your soul evolves, the energy of your soul can be more strongly seen and felt; it will feel more electrifying to the person who comes near you, especially if you have a similar spiritual awareness. Some people can also see your aura; the energy field that surrounds the human body and all living things. This aura can also be seen by other methods as well.

Everything about us can also be seen in our aura by spiritually enlightened entities, such as our Ascended Master type guides. It is impossible to hide anything about our past or present life from them; they are the all-knowing and all-seeing entities of all that is, ever was, and ever will be.

After our soul leaves our current physical body to move into Heaven it will take on a new physical body that resembles the current one; usually that body will look younger than the one on Earth when you relocate to Heaven but, as always, your soul remains the same soul.

We can assist our 'self,' our soul, and our soul's evolutionary process by the way we think and live. It is beneficial to assist our soul in moving to the highest spiritual level possible before the soul is ready to vacate the physical body and move into Heaven.

As I always say, 'like attracts like,' therefore your spiritual level at the time you leave the physical body determines the level you relocate to in Heaven for additional learning and evolving.

Our soul leads us through life with its built-in Soul Guidance System, SGS for short. We are all here on Earth at this time for a specific mission; we were each assigned a project before we came here.

No matter how many physical bodies we take on during reincarnations, our SGS is the tool we use to accomplish our mission. The physical vehicle allows the soul to be in the right place at just the right time in order to fulfill a mission that you came into this physical body for.

Our life's mission moves along faster if we pay attention to the guidance that our SGS shares with us. I didn't know what my mission was early in life but my soul did; the soul never forgets, it is omnipresent in our lives at all times. I continued in life with what my physical body/brain wanted me to do until I realized that method was not balanced and therefore wasn't working smoothly.

We exist in a physical body, in part, for the learning process that helps us to evolve spiritually. When all of our souls who have split off have achieved their completed higher consciousness they will come back together as one powerful force. I actually feel this is the reason for the split to begin with because the soul can gain more spiritual power with this process, an energy that is closest to the energy of God or the God Source.

Spiritual growth is a pleasant experience and many businesses are even beginning to notice that allocating meditation time for their employees is helpful. Many medical physicians are now saying that meditation is good for your health for several reasons; many are starting to see 'the light' through the health benefits of meditation.

In order for us to achieve a more powerful knowingness we need to allow time for our spiritual growth. We can enjoy life and the ability to expose ourselves to the higher power while in a physical body; this can be done through a variety of forms of meditation.

We live in a physically-minded planet, which makes it harder to evolve spiritually; in a way this is part of our test here on Earth. Our brain wants to be the ruler of our life and sometimes it becomes too much in control when we are more focused on the physical plane of existence than we are on the soul/spiritual part of life. This causes the soul to function less in our lives; it is the brain battling the soul body. The brain wants to win.

Life flows so much smoother when using our SGS more than the brain. My experiences have been that when I think with my soul everything works out naturally and as it was intended; with the brain, not so much!

It seems that our soul growth in this day and age has been pushed to the side for the sake of living more in the physical and material realm. We are also exposed to a lot more violence and negativity than we were in the past due to technology. All of these things deter our spiritual growth.

We have the tools within us for raising our consciousness, or our soul's spiritual level. We can use meditation, spend time with spiritual studies that we are led to, and you may even have a spiritual intervention by one of your guides; all of these are tools to reach a higher spiritual level in our soul.

We all have guides, even if we don't know it yet or talk about it publicly. A lot of people sweep those experiences under the rug because it is not a mainstream conversation and doesn't fit in with society as much as it should; although it is getting more accepted at this time. I know this because I used to be one of those people who kept my spiritual life in the closet. I have met many people who have confided in me about their spiritual experiences but they are still in the closet.

You can manifest a certain amount of a higher consciousness just by desiring it. The more emotion and desire you put into any one thing, the more you will manifest. You can also manifest material things in your life with the same process. We all have that power; we just have to allow it and practice with it.

Our intended master plan in life is to manifest a higher level of consciousness, as opposed to manifesting material things. We can do both but they should be kept equal for the balance. It is very easy to get out of balance when manifesting the material things in our lives becomes the main focus. Once you focus on raising your consciousness the rest will fall into place and you will automatically be taken care of: you will have what you need and more.

Just the other day, I was reflecting on how lucky I have been to be able to let my higher consciousness guide me to the things that have recently worked well financially for me. At that time, I received a telepathic message, "When you work for the God source, God works for you." I rest my case.

## Topic # 9:  Kirlian Photography

I received additional confirmation that the soul body and the physical body are separate when I was led to have my picture taken using Kirlian photography; it uses a type of camera that photographs both your aura and your physical body at one time.

We actually have a light around our body called an aura. I don't normally see auras but I know many that do. I have seen proof of the soul's aura when I was able to see my physical and soul body in the Kirlian photograph.

I saw other photographs on display there and noticed that each and every aura or soul body looked different. Each soul is obviously individual but an enlightened Native American woman once told me that she does see auras and the larger the aura the more spiritually evolved that person is.

The Kirlian photo gives you the visual and an AH HA moment that confirms that we really do have these two bodies.  I could now see it as well as sensing its presence with me at all times. If you can see auras with the naked eye, Kirlian photos would not be such a revelation to you.

For me it was helpful to see this aura on a photo; it drove the point home and it will forever be my understanding that the soul can actually be seen and is separate from the body.

## Topic # 10:  The Soul and Body Separately in Action

I later had another experience that confirmed the soul and body as being two separate things; as if that photo session wasn't proof enough for me. A lot of the information I share has been gained through my guides creating circumstances for me to experience; within each experience there was always a teaching.

The events that were created in my life were seemingly coincidental events that were far too numerous to be coincidental. As it turned out in my life, these coincidences were nothing more than my fate: the fate that defined my mission of sharing what I have learned. I never cease to be amazed with these events. Some of them are so bizarre I can barely believe my eyes when I experience them.

In one of those almost unbelievable experiences, I again was shown that the soul and physical body are separate although they are housed together and work together while we are living. I know this sounds like an obviously simple statement but the visual reality of this event drove the point home for me and gave it additional clarity.

Several of my relatives had come for a visit at my Mother's home for a small reunion; there were probably about ten family members who were sitting in the living room at the time the event occurred. We were chatting away and all of a sudden every person in the room disappeared all at once and right before my very eyes, their physical bodies had just instantly vanished. I was shocked and wondered if I was in a twilight zone because all that was left of their physical body was their soul in the exact place where their body was sitting a few seconds ago.  After the physical bodies had vanished I actually saw the soul of each person sitting there in a chair without a body!

About as quickly as I realized that I was looking at their souls, their physical bodies appeared again in the same exact spot; it was as if they had never really left.

I now realize that this situation was created for me so that it would be clear in my mind that the physical body and the soul are two separate things. This event was probably one of my most interesting experiences to date.

## Topic # 11:  The Third Eye

During another one of my bizarre experiences, I learned about x-ray vision.   I had been in an auto accident at that time; I had a minor injury to the cervical spine. I was hospitalized and in traction due to this injury.

Throughout my hospital stay, the nurses periodically came in to check on me as I was alone in the hospital room. The nurses had always kept the door to my room closed for peace and quiet in my room. I had to wear a thick, black mask to block the bright lights of the hallway for the times when the door to my room was opened.

Near the end of my week in traction, I had a weird experience that was new to me. I was meditating and working on healing myself and had fallen asleep when all of a sudden someone opened my hospital door without knocking. I saw the nurse standing in the doorway as the brilliant hallway lights blared behind her.

After she left the room I realized that I still had the mask on when I saw her standing in the doorway, I had seen her as clearly as if I had no mask on at all. It was definitely an X-ray vision experience. I kept telling myself that logically speaking this can't possibly happen; so one day I tried to see through the mask in bright sunlight, I couldn't see a thing.

Each time I doubt some of these unusual experiences they seem to happen again just to prove to me that I wasn't hallucinating. Other times I will get confirmation and proof in another manner to reassure me that it really did happen.  After years of doubting these events I accepted them more as fact but I am still a very skeptical person about most everything.

Holding true to my usual scenario of learning through the teachings of my guides I had a second x-ray vision during meditation, this time I was able to see through the ceiling and into the night sky filled with stars.  It shocked me so much that the x-ray vision came to a halt and I was once again staring at the ceiling.

Today as I started to write this chapter, both the x-ray vision experiences flashed before my eyes and a major revelation was given to me; in a flash I had the knowingness that we have a 'third eye.' This third eye actually sees things as clear or more so than the eyes in our physical body; it works in conjunction with the soul and can actually kick in to witness things when necessary. The third eye has x-ray vision and can see through solid objects, much like our soul can travel through anything solid. The soul and the third eye have unlimited abilities; together they are the real self.

When your soul is more fully active, the function of the third eye can be more fully active. When you soul travel, the third eye is functioning fully, just like the soul is; the soul replaces the physical body and the third eye replaces the normal eyesight of the physical body. Together they can see the other side of the veil or into another dimension.

This x-ray vision experience just added another missing piece to the puzzle of life.

## Topic #12:  The SGS, Our Soul Guidance System

Other than the connection I felt with something out in the universe at an early age, all I understood about life was the information I received from my elders. They taught that we are born, we live, and die and then we will wait in our grave until Jesus comes back to get us. At that point Jesus will take us to Heaven. Never did I hear that we could go back and forth to Heaven for visits or that each of us has a soul that guides us through life. It was all about Jesus or God doing everything for us instead of each of us progressing with our soul guidance. There is so much more for us to participate in than what I was taught.

As I became an adult, my life was very hectic, juggling several careers at one time; I was basically too scattered to realize that there was anything to life other than working, sleeping, eating, having a busy social life and eventually dying. That is what I was taught and therefore I lived it. Then a calling came over me but I didn't know what it was. I realized that my life was going nowhere except to repeat the same thing I did yesterday, it was like a treadmill; I was going nowhere and things were not working smoothly.

I started to wonder, what is the point of life? There has to be more to it than this, this type of life makes no sense. That was the time I knew it was time to discover why I was here and if I had a mission. I stopped everything I was doing with my life and went into isolation for three days of meditation. On the third day I emerged knowing what my missions were.

There is more than one part to this mission; part of it is to share the treasure of information I've received from my spiritually enlightened guides and soul experiences in this lifetime. The other part of the mission is in the planning stage at this time and hopefully will begin in the near future. It is important to use the brain and soul together when venturing into a new project and I will definitely be working in that manner.

Even if we don't know what our mission is yet, our soul does; our soul has the entire blueprint imbedded within it and it is always there for us to tap into.   The soul will give you the clues and guidance along the way and all you have to do is allow, pick up on them and then to follow the promptings in order to be in the right

27

place at just the right time. This is part of your soul's evolutionary process.

As previously discussed, the soul exudes a spiritual energy that can be felt by others, each with its own identity. That energy is quickly felt when you meet someone, it either repels you or you feel the balance of energies between the two of you. You are feeling the soul's spiritual aura and energy. If it is a positive or balanced feeling that means you are on similar spiritual level to that person or they could even be a parallel soul if strongly magnetized to them.

When a spiritual guide approaches me for communication or to do healing on me I recognize them by their soul's energy; that is how I know who they are if they are not in full solid physical body. It is that same type energy connection you feel when you walk up to someone and feel their energy. The big difference is that a spiritual guide's energy is vibrating at a higher frequency than people living on Earth; their energy is very powerful, balanced, and electrifying, exuding pure love. My soul recognized them and I always feel a connection with them; I feel as though I am a part of them.

In most cases, I have found that I already knew my guides before coming to Earth this time and previously had a strong connection with them before this lifetime; therefore I recognize them and feel that I am a part of them. It makes that recognition instantly easier because I quickly know who they are. This is a little different than when I meet someone in a physical body and feel some kind of a connection with them because there are always some elements of mystery as to how I knew them before.

## Topic # 13:  Energy, Vibrational Frequency, Dimensions and Raising Consciousness

I learned that everything is energy, even God. Everything operates at a specific vibrational frequency. Anything can become more or less visible to the naked eye in a split second if that frequency changes.  When it slows down it becomes more visible, when it speeds up it becomes invisible. There are various dimensions all around us that we do not see; this is because they are vibrating at a different frequency than we are.

I also learned that by focusing on raising the level of our soul's consciousness or spiritual levels through various forms of meditation, we are able to connect with God's energy as well as with those who are now residents of Heaven while we are living in this lifetime. With each meditative process you retain part of the higher consciousness level you gain bit by bit because it accumulates and elevates your consciousness permanently. Raising our spiritual energy level is like slowly turning up a dimmer switch on a light.

With pure intentions we can also connect with beings that are in a higher spiritual plane of existence besides Heaven. We can view the events going on in that location at that time and sometimes even participate in the goings-on as they are happening. You will then return to your earthly body after an experience like this. It is very safe due to the silver cord.

When this has happened for me, my soul comes back to my physical body on Earth and sometimes forgets all about what just happened until sometime later when I relax. When we relax, our brain is more open and we can make that recall.  If you plan to do this you should keep a journal because writing it down as soon as you recall it helps to plant the experience solidly in the brain; otherwise you may never recall it until years later because it was a soul experience not a mental process.

In order to create a simple explanation about the location of Heaven and other dimensions, I will give you an analogy. If you mixed oil and water you would see that it doesn't mix; it ends up in layers. Dimensions exist as if they are in layers; they don't mix. Again, we exist in one dimension and don't see the other dimensions all around us due to frequency variations.

Heaven is located in a different dimension than we are. You can visit your friends and family who are in Heaven while you are still living on Earth. Heaven is not the only dimension that exists out there. Each dimension is separate from the other and each one resonates at a different vibrational frequency, therefore we don't normally see the different dimensions with the naked eye as I explained earlier. That analogy pretty much describes what I have witnessed as to how the layers of dimensions actually exist and function.

The God-like spiritual guides use their soul capabilities to travel to various dimensions that we do not see with the naked eye. They adjust their frequency at will so they can visit other dimensions. In reality the things they manifest, such as a change is frequency is done by desire, a thought, it seems to be instantaneous for them. With these changes, their physical bodies can appear or disappear instantly and roam to any place they want to go. I have witnessed them change solidity right before my eyes. Everything they do is done in a flash; my brain can barely keep up with their changes because of the speed in which they function during the times that they have visited with me.

The spiritual love energy on the Earth is far from being as powerful as that of God's love energy at the God Source. Nature is actually closer to that higher love energy than we are because it isn't of the physical/materialistic nature; it is just happy being nature and you can feel the peacefulness coming from it.

The higher we go in the various dimensions, the higher the spiritual energy is at that location. When you get through all of the layers you know that you have reached the God Source. The energy in that dimension is an all-consuming pure love energy that functions there. This is where the God-consciousness perfected resides, and where the answers to everything can be found. It is the location I ended up at the day I saw 'all that is.'

When I meditate I like to view that space as a ball of white light in the sky. I project my intention to reach the white light that is the God-consciousness in order to receive the answer I need, resolve a situation or receive a healing.

Once you truly tap into that highest spiritual level or God-Source you can quickly bring a problem into that zone and the problem will be resolved. It doesn't work if you are dwelling on the problem during the meditation, you must bring it in at the moment you feel you are up to the highest level possible for it to work in perfection. That sounds easier than it actually is; our mind tends to get in the way and bring us back to Earth so the brain can tell us what to do next.

I have found that life, my body, and my mission functions much better when I can spend equal time both with the physical and the soul bodies; in other words, I devote half of my time to working on evolving spiritually and the other half to dealing with the physical matters at hand. Spending time with my guides is also helpful as their energy is pure love energy; it is so balanced that it helps to balance me. Living my life is like living with one foot on Earth's soil and the other foot in the spiritual worlds or dimensions, living in or between many worlds.

To move forward with the raising of consciousness and achieving our goals the fastest method is to slow down and 'be in the moment.' Be present in each action, allow, and 'just be.' To accomplish this, we must let go of agonizing about past events and worrying about the future. When we live life in this manner it allows us to be in the right place at just the right time; it's magical.

## Topic # 14: Teachings from the Other Side

I had two visits from my dad after his death. The first one was brief, but the second one was very lengthy.

My dad was not exempt from spiritual experiences involving those who had passed on, though he would never talk about it to anyone except the family. On one occasion he saw his mother walk through the living room while she was actually on her deathbed in the bedroom and not up physically walking around. This event occurred about the time that they found out she had passed on in her sleep. I felt his experience occurred so he would learn that there is life after death.

He came to me for a visit several years after his departure from Earth. I feel that his visit finally came about because I had frequently wondered why he had not paid a visit to me already. I wasn't sure he would ever pay me a visit considering the length of time since he had passed. Most of my friends and family who had passed on paid a visit to me shortly after their passing.

He visited me on the first occasion while I was driving in my car. This time he had come to clear up something about the details of a previous health problem that he had before he passed away, something that I had not understood previously. This message gave me the clarity I needed for a better understanding of him and his health.

His long delay before visiting me was most likely because he was tied up with studying and progressing in spirit. When he was alive, he didn't have much time to spend with the family or pursuing a spiritual life. He had several occupations at once, which left no time for him to slow down and smell the roses.

He came to me once again a few years later. This visit came at a time when I had reclined to read a book. At first, I didn't realize that it was him; I didn't know what was going on. His visit was totally different than my other visits with those who had passed on had been. This time, it was as if there was a movie screen in the room and a movie appeared out of thin air and started playing. I was not aware of anything else in the room as this movie started to roll.

It is hard to say how long this movie lasted, but it was very lengthy in content. It was long enough that a feature film could be made from all of the things that I saw. The content was educational and had an inspiring message. The interesting thing about this movie was the way the end of it was shown to me; a television appeared on the big screen that the movie was playing on. It looked like the one in my living room. It was as if the big screen disappeared and the rest of the movie was shown to me on this second screen that had appeared. At that point, my dad appeared on the television screen just long enough for him to deliver the last few sentences of the movie. Needless to say, I was quite amazed with what had transpired; it taught me a lot and gave me a new appreciation for counting the moments in life and being in the moment more often.

The movie was filled with detailed events that had played out in our family life over a number of years. In a nutshell it portrayed what my dad learned after he was in Heaven and had a chance to look back at his Earth life; you know what they say about hindsight.

It was a great film and a moving story, one that everybody should see in order to appreciate the real things in life, as opposed to being in 'social consciousness mode' too often. It was also very unique in the way it had been plotted. And of course there was a twist to the movie that you wouldn't see coming. Only my dad would want to portray these events to me to get his message across; it was a teaching for me but applies to everyone on Earth. The message was a powerful one that should be portrayed in a real film.

This visit with my dad had a prominent viewpoint regarding living in the moment and how important it is to 'just be' and allow while we have the opportunity in this lifetime. It just goes to show you that we learn in unexpected ways; we just have to pay attention to the teachings we receive regarding living life to the fullest to achieve a higher spiritual awareness.

After the movie he created had ended, I knew that I was supposed to have the story produced for the public. Since the last part of it was shown on a television screen, it seemed to suggest that it should be shown as a television show, where more people would be able to see it than in a theater. It was too long and detailed for a one-time television show, although it could be a miniseries or a full-length movie. It is an important message that will help others on their path through life as well as their life after death.

I have always kept a tape recorder and notebook nearby because of the huge number of unusual events that happen in my life. I could never have remembered all of the details of my dad's movie without my trusty notes and recordings. Thank goodness, I had fresh batteries during the lengthy details of the movie. This movie is still on my list of things to do.

## Topic # 15:  Reincarnation

Reincarnation is the process through which many master type guides have evolved; they have completed their spiritual missions and lessons learned while in a physical body. This is how they have achieved their higher consciousness and mastered the many powers that they possess; they became Ascended Masters: masters of a highly elevated consciousness.

There are many of them who exist in various dimensions and move in and out of those dimensions at will; they can do this because they have achieved that greatness and ability. I know because I personally have had meetings with a lot of them. They have powers beyond comprehension and possess a God-like essence that is indescribable in human terms.

These all-powerful entities have the ability to move in and out of their physical bodies at will also. They can be present with me in the physical or in a spirit or soul light body. It is very common for them to make these adjustments in a flash and at will.

Not everyone believes in reincarnation but that is what makes the world go around. Earth is the free will planet; it is our choice to have our own belief system and total free will. I am telling my story and my beliefs as I have learned them from my experiences in life with the most highly evolved spiritual teachers that are not incarnated on Earth at this time. I also have had several past lives that I have recalled throughout this lifetime, so I am definitely a believer in reincarnation.

I read a book that told about a spiritually evolved man who saw himself in another lifetime with the exact physical appearance in this lifetime.  I don't know if that is true but it is interesting that we look the same in Heaven as we do on Earth, except for the fact that we are much younger when we are in Heaven, from what I have witnessed.

I have seen myself in past lives with the current family members that I have in this lifetime and they looked like they do now, with age differences of course. I have also met people on Earth in this lifetime and later had visions of a past life with those same individuals. Two of them remembered the same past life with me as well; in fact, one of them approached me about this before I actually had the experience of seeing that lifetime with him. As it turned out with both individuals, we had the same physical look as we do in this lifetime, but that's not to say that this is always the case.

I also had a rather unique visit from a woman who said she knew me from one of my past incarnations; she was not an individual living on Earth at this time. This visit occurred during a morning meditation when I felt a sudden burst of spiritual energy in the room. Quickly, a lady appeared beside me and looked me right in the face. I saw her in the same manner as I see my guides; she was in her light body.

I thought for sure I was in the twilight zone for a minute or two. She started to speak telepathically and said, "Well, you're — — aren't you?" She was calling me by a name that wasn't mine, a name that I recognized from history class.

I couldn't deny her powerful, female presence as she stood there, no matter what name she called me. She continued to speak loud and clear with a very strong British accent, and she went on to tell me that she had known me from a past life. In this particular past life, I had been a well-known historical male figure who had played a major part in the history of the United States.

Needless to say, I was shocked about the facts she gave me, but they also made a lot of sense because I had previously visited one of the locations where this historical figure had been during his lifetime. At that time I felt a strong emotional connection to him and the events there but I didn't understand why at that time.

She was surprised that I didn't recognize her, and that I didn't know about my past life as this male figure. She quickly created a movie-like vision for me. I watched myself make history in this past life while the movie rolled right before my eyes.

She also informed me about one of my missions on Earth that was yet to come in this lifetime. This particular mission was to be connected with that past life. In my mind, I assumed that this was why she had appeared there in my home.

With all of this information at hand, I became very curious as to who she was, so I asked what her name was. Just then, a tangible, solid ink pen and a lined tablet of white paper magically appeared right out of thin air. I was mesmerized by all of this, but I was still listening and watching intently.

Her answer was revealed to me as she used the pen to write her name across the lined tablet that she had just created. As it floated across the paper, she wrote the word 'Bridges' in fancy script. Her handwriting was beautiful. It was very ornate and artistic.

I have not confirmed all that she had to say just yet, however, I intend to follow up on this and see where it takes me. I was surprised and amazed by her visit but this event gave me even more confirmation that reincarnation is a fact of nature.

## Topic # 16:  A Soul in Action

I met two people I knew in a past life one day when my friend Sue and I went to downtown Orlando for a jewelry show. The minute I was in the door, it felt like a big, unstoppable hand was guiding me until I reached the right place at just the right time. As we reached the top floor and made a left we went straight to the booth run by a man named Tom and his wife, Peggy. When Sue and I met this couple we quickly became best friends; we were practically inseparable for years.

Tom was a very creative guy, very artistic, and he worked as a custom jewelry designer. He was very laid back as if he never had a care in the world; he leaned toward being a hippie, which was really in at that time.

After a few years of friendship with Tom and Peggy they got divorced but we still hung out as a group. I find it interesting to meet people from our past lives. With some, it is a quick meeting to work out the previous life's karma; with others, it is a long drawn out set of experiences, which was the case with Tom. Meeting Tom gave me my first opportunity to work in the jewelry designing field with him but that was only a small part of the experiences we had together.

After many years of fun with Tom and Peggy, Tom suddenly became very ill. The last time Sue and I saw him was at the hospital where he was heavily sedated and things did not look good for his recovery. Sue sensed how grave his illness was the minute she saw him on the hospital bed and she almost passed out.

It wasn't long until I received a phone call from Peggy to tell me that he had passed away. Shortly after his death, he paid a visit to me at my home. He said, "Please come to see me at the funeral home; bring only one white rose and place it across my chest. I don't want a lot of flowers. I did not want to be laid out at a funeral home, either; I wanted to be cremated."

I told Peggy about the things Tom had told me. I explained that he wanted to be cremated. She gasped and looked as though she was in complete shock. She was very upset because she had already made all of the arrangements for him at the funeral home. There was to be no cremation. It was too late to change anything.

All of the sudden, she recalled that when he was sick he had told her that he wanted to be cremated if he died. He had also told her that he wanted his ashes sprinkled at sea. He had served in the US Navy when he was younger. I asked her why she had not granted his wish. She said that she thought he was just talking out of his head due to being so ill and on so many drugs for pain. She went on to tell me that he had also come to her after his death to give her a similar message. He told her to bring only one red rose and lay it across his chest. I had a strong spiritual connection with both Tom and Peggy, which accounted for many of the happenings in our lives, both before and after his death.

Years later, I ran into Peggy. We had lost track of each other after Tom's death. I had no idea where she lived at that time but I had been thinking about her almost every day. I pulled into the parking lot of a health food store that I rarely shopped at. I was sitting in the car and reviewing my shopping list when I happened to look up and there she was, walking right in front of my car; I couldn't believe my eyes. After all of this time, what a coincidence! I quickly called out to her so we could catch up on everything. During our visit she told me that she was remarried and now had a baby.

We made arrangements for another visit and she brought her baby along. As I held her baby girl, I could sense that this baby was different than most. She had an aura of energy around her that made her feel like an Angel. I had never had that kind of feeling with a baby before. She was glowing and felt weightless, as if she was floating. That was a very unusual experience for me.

During my visit with Peggy, I remembered that I had previously had a premonition that Tom was going to reincarnate and come back to her. When I told her about this, she looked surprised. She told me that she had had the same premonition. I guess she realizes now that Tom would stop at nothing to get back to her, even coming back as a girl to win her love.

It was clear to me that meeting this couple with a past life connection to me was part of the teachings I received; it showed me there is life before and after death, and proved to me that it is possible to visit with those who have passed on.

We definitely never lose touch with friends and family after their death. They are never far away; they are right there on the other side of the veil. We can visit with them outside Earth periodically throughout our life if we understand the process in which life cycles function as I have outlined in this book. If you understand how this life process works, it will allow you to let your walls down that have blocked you from visiting with them. They may have wanted to come to you but didn't act upon it because they didn't want to frighten you. Of course, this doesn't apply to every living person because there are so many enlightened people on Earth that have not had their guard up, so to speak.

You will continue to have other incarnations with those you have unfinished business with; this is not to say that every incarnation is for that purpose because you might be sent on a mission that has nothing to do with your past life connections with others. Recollections that I have had of my various incarnations with the same people in this lifetime have proven that to me. I am a firm believer that there are no mistakes in life when we follow our guidance.

## Topic # 17:  Inter-dimensional Travel and Time-Travel

I am not a scientist; therefore I will give you a simplified explanation of what occurs during my inter-dimensional travel and time-travel events.

Periodically, I do a type of travel that I call inter-dimensional travel: I am traveling outside the Earth's viewable dimension using my soul body. When I visit any dimension unseen with the naked eye here on Earth, I actually relocate to that dimension temporarily; I live the experience as if I am physically there living it in the moment, and then I return to my physical body.

Heaven is located in another dimension of reality, therefore when I visit that dimension it is considered inter-dimensional travel as well.  I have often visited many dimensions other than Heaven.

Residents of Heaven are doing inter-dimensional travel when they travel to visit us as well. While living in Heaven, they have a physical body and a soul, as I mentioned earlier. They use the soul to do this type of travel and then return to their physical body in the same manner that we do while living on Earth.  They can achieve this by focusing on the desire to visit someone in another dimension.

There are times when I also do what I call time-travel; I go to another space in time, so to speak, right here on Earth's viewable areas.  When I experience time-traveling here on Earth I also relocate to that area temporarily, just as I do during inter-dimensional travel.

The processes are the same except that sometime I am traveling outside Earth and other times I am traveling and end up in a different timeless-zone so to speak right here on Earth.

People on Earth experience time in a linear fashion even though there is really no such thing as time. Everything past, present, and future are all going on at the same time. So in essence, I travel into one of those timeless-zones, participate, and later come right back into my body in our current space and time as we know it. I am living the event as if it is occurring at that moment, just as I do in inter-dimensional travel.

In time-travel I always instinctively know if what I am experiencing is the past or a future time that is to come to us on Earth; again, my soul is in charge.

Sometimes I see something that would indicate a date that this particular event I am seeing will occur or if it has already occurred in our history. My guides often give me specific dates for events that are to come after I return from such an event as well.

When I go to a new time/space that is in our past, it has already been experienced in the past by others even though I am experiencing it as it is a current event.

If I travel to the future here on Earth I know it is the future although there may or may not be an indicator for the day or time that this particular event will occur in Earth time. If there is no time indicator for this travel event my guides are often around to give me additional information when I return to my body. If it's a future event that I experience, it will be experienced by others on Earth in their future.

When I return to my physical body, I realize that I have just lived the future or the past; therefore I know in advance what is going to happen in the future, or has happened in the past. This is how I often received information to share as a prediction for our future or make new discoveries in historical events.

This type of travel is very natural and easy if you allow yourself to 'just be' and let nature take its course; forget the fear and allow the moment. You can be living on Earth one moment then suddenly traveling to another dimension or to the past or future for a short period of time; it can take place in a split second.

These events have occurred during meditation and even when I am walking through the house while being spaced out; being spaced out is also a form of meditation. At these times my brain is inactive and not reminding me of what I need to do. The brain's silent times create great mediations because they allow the soul to take over and allow us to 'just be'; this is also a form of 'being in the moment.'

We will always come back to our body here on Earth when doing these travels because the soul is doing the traveling, not the physical body. Just as previously discussed, the soul can never permanently separate until the death process takes place.

There are many methods of doing time-travel. I didn't realize this before I actually experienced time-travel. In some cases, time-travel can automatically take place if your spiritual consciousness is at an evolutionary stage that allows for it. Your evolved spiritual guides may also assist in this travel process if they choose to send you on an adventure to bring information back to Earth. In addition, there is such a thing as a time-travel device to create and accelerate a time-travel experience.

Who says you can't take it with you?

One of my visits to Heaven that was very educational for me was when I paid a visit to my friend Tom whom I spoke about earlier. He was a resident of Heaven at the time of this event. I do not know for sure if he resides there now. A year or so after he died I had been traveling right here on Earth and working on a project at a location that Tom loved; he had also worked with me in that area in the past when he was living. I sensed his presence very strongly at the job location that day.

When I arrived back at my home in the middle of the afternoon I took my suitcase straight to the bedroom. I sat on the edge of the bed and threw my body backward onto the bed to relax. As I hit the bed, I recall staring at the ceiling for a second, and then I quickly zoomed out of my body. I went directly to a beautiful, peaceful city where I met eye-to-eye with Tom.

I could feel myself standing on a sidewalk as I spotted him at a distance. He walked down the sidewalk and straight toward me. I didn't see any other people there on the street. The place looked somewhat similar in structure to cities that we have here on Earth but it didn't feel the same. The buildings were very tall and seemingly endless as far as my eyes could see. They all seemed to be touching each other or were just very close together like apartment buildings.

It looked like a very big city with streets, although they were not actually streets but rather just a space between the building and the wide sidewalks. There were no motorized vehicles there in sight where our street would normally be. That space could be there for another purpose because I was very clear on the fact that there were no vehicles of transportation there; I didn't feel as though they had a need for them.

The sidewalks and buildings were a pale beige color. There was a brilliant white light that permeated and surrounded everything; it lit up the area in the same manner that our sun does. It was the same white light that is seen at the end of the tunnel by those that have a near-death experience. It was as if this white light was just part of the location, part of everything; I felt it had to do with the white light of God's essence that was just natural there. This white light seemed to cause a slight glow or sparkle to everything it permeated. It was as if there was a mist that was evenly distributed in the air; it seemed as though this misty look was due to the intensity of the white light. I could see everything very clearly from my vantage point, even though the white rays were shining brightly in, on, and around everything, including Tom. The light was so intense that I was amazed it didn't hurt my eyes even though it was the brightest and purist white I had ever seen.

I just stood there on the sidewalk mesmerized by all I saw. I looked ahead of me and saw that Tom was walking closer to me by that time. He walked with purpose and almost seemed to float along as if he were light as a feather although it was obvious that he was as solid as we are. When I first saw him I didn't think he realized that I was standing there because he was looking down at the sidewalk as if to watch his step. As he came closer, he looked me straight in the eye, and burst out in his familiar big smile when our eyes met.

He was always such a happy, carefree person. He seemed to enjoy every minute of life and never seemed to have a serious moment. He apparently hadn't changed according to the essence I sensed with him when he got closer to me—he didn't seem to have a care in the world.

There he was in Heaven, looking exactly the way he did when he was healthy. The only difference was that his deep smile-lines had disappeared or lessened, which made him look younger than when I knew him on Earth—at that time he was in his thirties. As he smiled, I could see that he still had the same crooked front tooth that he had when he was alive.

He wore a loose, white shirt like hippies used to wear. It hung about ten inches below the waistline and flowed in the breeze. He also wore sandals and a pair of white, loose-fitting pants.

Tom always had shoulder-length, blond hair that was slightly receding. Yes, he still had that same blonde hair, styled the same way but without the receding hairline. His hair gently blew in the breeze with the brilliant, white light shining through it, causing it to glow and sparkle.

I headed toward him to give him a hug when suddenly, I found myself back in my bedroom, still lying there on the bed and looking up at the ceiling. I had returned to my bedroom as quickly as I left it. What a neat experience!

After the fact, I had to laugh about seeing Tom in such a hippie-looking outfit because it was definitely something he would have worn in his earthly life. Who says you can't take it with you?

I wondered if I accidently had traveled into his space or if he created that event. Knowing Tom, I would have to say he created it. He had a way of making things happen; he had quite a gift for manifesting.

## Topic # 18:  Merging of a Soul

My guides also have a way of making things happen. It never ceases to amaze me when they are able to give me instructions to be in the right place at the right time, even though I have no idea what it will lead to at the time.

On one occasion, I begrudgingly carried out their instructions even though I really didn't want to go to this particular location. As usual this adventure created an amazing outcome and teaching.

Soon after I arrived at this location in the mountains I met with a man who was known by the title 'the man who fell from another planet.' His given name was Van. It became obvious to me after I had been guided to this new area that it was all in order to spend time with this enlightened man. He was a therapeutic body worker and had healed many people in his lifetime.

He had been paralyzed at one time and healed himself by using reflexology.  The next day he got out of bed and walked out of the hospital. This experience caused him to want to help and heal others. He also had several near-death experiences and returned to continue with raising his spiritual consciousness in this lifetime. He even healed another person who was unable to walk. During that experience the client was lying on the table while Van was doing his treatment and suddenly the client magically lifted off the table, stood upright and walked.

I was in need of his services so I booked a long series of treatments with him due to this track record. I had great improvements in my health and my spiritual development during the time of these treatments. Just being in his presence was such a peaceful and powerful experience, in addition to the benefits of the healing I received. During his treatments there was always a powerful electrifying spiritual energy transfer that was imparted to me from his higher consciousness.

During one of my treatments I had an unusual experience with him. Van said to me: "I see a brilliant, spiritual, white light energy that is beside you now. It is the One of your parallel souls that is part of the original of you, the One who has maintained its divinity, the One who possesses full Christ Consciousness and has never chosen to incarnate in a physical body. This One is now ready to merge with you, if you will permit it."

He went on to say, "You created or set all of these plans before incarnating; now, it is time. Your other parallel souls are having too great of a time in what they're doing to be interested in merging."

Van also explained to me that he would battle with this or any Entity/soul that was around me, and he would do it immediately and permanently remove it from my existence if he did not know for sure that it was my full Christ Consciousness he was dealing with. He assured me that this One particular soul was, in fact, who he said it was. My knowingness told me that this was all true as I recognized that energy, in other words it resonated with my soul. So of course, I agreed to the merging at that time.

I had previously been experiencing this merging process before he explained what it was, so now it all made sense. I didn't know why it was happening but accepted it because I felt a connection to it, as if it was a part of me! This seemed to fit in with what I had learned about each of us having only one soul that has split into more than one, yet we are still the same one soul as a whole, each one learning on its own.

Finally, I was able to put a lot of the teachings together; each was a piece of the puzzle of life which helped to complete the big picture for me regarding this particular situation.

The merging that Van spoke of is a merging of the souls. A soul merging is much more intense and powerful than an energy transfer for healing, but in reality they are both energy transfers of a sort. I now understand this merging process as a restructuring of my soul; in the past before I met Van, I thought it was just healing that is called restructuring. When the merging process is implemented, it is extremely intense and powerful. It feels like electricity penetrates every cell of my body at once. It is very tingly, and I can feel each cell being electrified, but it doesn't actually hurt. The tingling stays with each cell for a while, and then dissipates.

Van said the merging was slowly being assimilated into my entire being. He explained that the energy of a soul merging would be too intense and powerful from this type Christ Consciousness to be done all at once; the body would not be able to tolerate the intensity of it. Consequently, it would happen over time and many mergings would take place before this particular parallel soul would be completely merged. So far I have had so many that I have lost count.

Van explained to me that a merging of this type could take a long time, and the body would have to adjust to the process as it took place. Retaining less social consciousness and gaining more Christ Consciousness is my ultimate goal, so I am receiving my desire.

I decided to take my friend Cindy to see Van after my wonderful experiences with him and learning about the healing he had done on himself and one other person. Cindy was in a wheel chair and had not walked since she was a small child. It took some convincing but she finally agreed, as I was sure she would receive some benefit from his treatment. I had it in my mind that she would get up and walk because of his track record.

We arrived for her appointment at Van's office, she got on the therapy table, and while she was in the middle of her treatment, Van quickly looked up from his work in surprise. He said, "Jesus is standing beside you, Cindy. He wants you to get up and walk." I was elated; my plan was working, but my heart quickly sank when she replied, "No, I want to heal myself. I will do it my way." Again, there is that free will, and it was not her will or her way to be healed at that time. I didn't get my way, but I understood that it was her choice to make, not mine. My motto is 'life is an alone process,' and that certainly applied here. That experience was worth the trip even though I didn't get my way.

Both Cindy and I became aware that we had a parallel life. In addition to what Van had told me, I had also been told by one of my guides that I also have a parallel life that is incarnated at this time and is living in the United States now. I actually know who she is but as far as I know she does not know me. She also works in the new age genre.

My friend Cindy saw one of her parallel lives who is currently living on Earth in a different country. A parallel soul can be anywhere and still join up again with the other parallel soul or souls when the time is right.

Even though we may be living in another location we still have that soul connection; it will never change because we are each a part of the same soul. If you wake up one morning in an unusual mood, and you find no reason for it, then one of your parallel lives may be having a bad day or an extra great day. If we do not focus on the rare mood and stay focused on our soul body and its guidance, that feeling will dissipate.

### Topic # 19:  Unseen Protectors

I will be forever grateful for the knowledge and other benefits I have received through the guidance I have received. It has helped me to evolve spiritually; I have gained knowledge about life's evolutionary system and the true nature of reality, not the reality that many of us were programmed with. In addition, I have received so much protection that it is obvious that there is something powerful at work here.

On more than one occasion, these unseen spiritual sources who protect me have found it necessary to physically take control of a specific situation to protect me from grave danger or even death.

I have often said, "I feel like I am now living my ninth life." I have never judged these events or questioned who my protectors were due to the fact these events were always positive and often time very miraculous; this was just a normal way of life for me. I want to acknowledge these beings because without them I wouldn't be here writing this book to help others.

 I spent many years arguing with myself about the validity of how I was able to have visits in Heaven and have some of those residents of Heaven pay a visit to me because this isn't supposed to happen according to the religious teachings I received in my early years. But no matter how I argued with myself they continued to happen; therefore, I finally realized that they were real. In more recent years these beings have made themselves more known to me on a personal basis, which has strengthened my faith. Thank God, many people are now seeing the light, literally, and not afraid to speak about this subject in public.

An interesting thing I have noticed when I return to Earth after having a visit in Heaven is that I feel a lot of negativity in the Earth's energy, as opposed to the balanced God-like love energy that exists in Heaven.

When I am on Earth most of the time I don't notice the energy as being negative because I am used to it. It may not feel negative to most people if they are in it all of the time but there is a major shift into a higher spiritual energy level when going into a dimension, such as Heaven. As our soul evolves, this positive love energy is our reward.

**Topic # 20:  Saved by an Unseen Entity**

There have been numerous times when I have been saved from accidents or things of that nature by an unseen presence. They have either made things happen to protect me or telepathically told me to do a certain thing. One instance was when I stayed overnight at a friend's house that was about thirty minutes from my home. I had to get up early the next morning to drive home without much sleep.

While driving, I realized that I had driven several miles down the wrong road. The road I found myself on took me about twenty or thirty minutes out of my way. I didn't remember turning onto this road or driving the distance. I have no idea how it happened. It was as if I was not even present in my body, mind, or spirit. I basically had lost time. I just all of a sudden became aware that I was still driving and knew I was on the wrong road. Then I had a flashback to an early morning vision I had that same day; it was like watching a movie. I recalled the entire vision. I had totally forgotten about the vision one second after I had seen it; I was barely awake at the time.

As the entire vision flashed before my eyes once again exactly as I had seen it the first time, I saw the front page of the local newspaper. In the lower-right corner of the page, I saw my bright orange Firebird totally wrecked, smashed all the way around and on the top. The newspaper story said I had missed the curve and rolled down the hill. There it was in full color: one big, crumpled, orange pile.

If my car had not taken the wrong road, I would normally have driven around this same curve in the news story to get to my destination. I feel quite sure I would have had the accident if I had continued on that road. An unseen force took over and saved me. This was one more time that I thanked God for all of my blessings; one of my powerful guides was watching over me once again

Another odd aspect of this incident was that the curve my car missed in the vision was within a minute or so of the place where I lived for many years. I have negotiated that curve many times without accident; it was very familiar to me.

I was happy to continue down the wrong road to get home. Those extra minutes to get home safely became a nonissue; time was no longer of the essence at that point.

I never really knew who saved my life that day nor did I inquire about it as this event occurred before I ever knew there was such a thing as a highly evolved, spiritually enlightened protector existed, other than Jesus. This incident fits right in with all of the other magical manifestation, protection, and guidance that I have been privileged to throughout my life.

The unseen aspects of life are much more complex than any of us know or realize, probably even me. I have been through so many different unknown and mysterious processes that were governed by the sometimes-unseen spiritual world. I don't doubt that there are many more mysteries that will be unveiled to me as well.

## Topic # 21: Near-Death Experience and Robert's Return

In 1970, I experienced what it's like to die through a near-death experience, also known as NDE. Since it was such a powerful spiritual experience, I have kept it fairly private.

After this experience, I read a lot of metaphysical books to learn more about what had actually happened to me. I learned that NDEs are very real and have been experienced by many. In a true near-death episode, a person actually dies. His or her soul or spirit body leaves the physical body. Then sometime later, it returns to the physical body and resumes living.

My NDE was different than most, but there was a teaching in it, like all my experiences. It occurred while I was sitting in the car at a drive-in theater with my husband, Robert. As a funeral scene progressed in the movie, I watched the hearse drive down a bumpy road with the casket inside. I suddenly left my body and went into the casket. In the beginning, I felt each bump of the road as I lay on the satin lining.

When I found myself there, my first thought was, "Wow, I'm dead! This is neat." I was glad I was dead, because I had such a calm, joyous, spiritual feeling of being at-one with God. Then I realized that I no longer had the aches and pains I had been experiencing for a couple of years due to severe anemia. It was strange to be free of pain and other bodily sensations so instantly.

The feelings were much the same as when I paid visits to friends and family in Heaven; it gave me a sense of relief and freedom from stress, as if I could finally relax and not have a care in the world. I knew I was dead and at the same time I was still alive and existing in a spirit world and no longer on Earth. I didn't feel as though I had gone all the way to Heaven though.

I quickly realized it doesn't hurt to die. I felt great. There was no hot and no cold; the temperature was neutral. I found it extremely comfortable to be dead. The death process was so effortless; one minute, I was alive, and the next second, I was dead.

After a period of time out of my body, I left the peaceful, silent environment and abruptly slammed back into my physical body with a jolt. For a split second, I was surprised at finding myself back in the car. The next thing I noticed was the loud, noisy, theater speakers blaring. This horrible noise was a shock to my entire being after coming back from such a peaceful silence. I came back into my physical body in a very harsh manner.

My attention was quickly diverted to Robert, who sat there crying. He was normally not the kind of person to let me see him be emotional; of course, he wasn't expecting me to see him crying, either.

I asked him what was wrong, because at that moment, I had no memory of what had happened to me. He said he thought I was dead. He said my eyes had been wide open and frozen in place. He had waved his hand in front of my eyes, I didn't blink, and he couldn't detect a breath. He had been afraid to touch me for fear I would fall over. I was puzzled and didn't know why he'd thought I was dead. It was strange that I could have forgotten that quickly about being in the casket.

We went right back to watching the movie and didn't discuss the incident again that evening. The next day as I was walking through the house, I flashed back on the entire event. I had a total recollection of what had happened the night before. Each and every detail of my NDE had been regained and I was again puzzled by the fact that I could have forgotten that I had briefly deceased.

After writing about my NDE, I started to question it. I vividly recalled the incident in detail, I knew it happened just as I explained…but did I really die? Was this some kind of experience to show me what takes place when a human dies? Was it a healing or all of those things? If I were actually dead, why would I go into a casket in a movie? Wouldn't I just go to a heavenly place and talk to a Being who would have a discussion with me as some others have done during an NDE? I have no answers to all of these questions at the moment, but what I do know for sure is that the experience taught me what it's like to die.

My NDE was very real for me and for my husband as well at that time, however, that really didn't convince him that there really is a Heaven or that there is life after death. He knew something weird had happened but he was pretty used to unusual events around me anyway, so to him it was just another one of those events, at least as far as he cared to admit.

Robert continued with not believing in anything that he couldn't see or touch. He was still afraid of my spiritual gifts after he witnessed my NDE; he didn't understand what it was all about.

At that stage of his life he had no belief system. He spent his early years in a religious school environment. My metaphysical life was so foreign to him because he had been programmed in the similar manner I had been as a child.

He later went into the military and lost faith in everything. I don't think he even believed in God at that point. He said, "I saw my friends die in the military. If God is good and in control of everything, then why would He let this happen?" Robert had witnessed and experienced one thing and was taught another. He seemed to have adopted the idea that all of his religious teachings had been a lie due to his confusion on these matters.

We were together for many years and eventually divorced. As he grew older, he wasn't as afraid to talk about my gift of intuition and my spiritual experiences; in the past, he avoided any conversation about anything spiritual, religious, or supernatural. Years after our divorce, he began to joke about me being psychic almost every time we had a conversation, which was frequent, as we stayed friends after our divorce. The subject usually came up because when I spoke with him I still knew everything that was going on in his life without having a way to know any of it, as I didn't speak with anybody that he knew and he didn't live near me at that time. Every time I called him, it seemed that it was always at a time when something was going on with him, or there was something that I needed to know about or get confirmation on. Years earlier this kind of thing would have spooked him, but by that time he had gotten pretty used to it.

Then one day, just recently, I had a very unusual experience with Robert; I  had done my morning stretches and was ready for breakfast, when out of the blue he was physically right there in my home with me. It was like going from one world and into another without knowing how I got there. When I realized that I was physically with him, a series of conversations took place and I knew we were back in a relationship again. This time, we had resolved everything that was ever a problem between us, now being in perfection; we were both very happy about it.

Then, all of the sudden he was no longer in my presence. I found myself in my home alone and realized that something strange had happened. I didn't understand what had happened at that moment so I just passed it off and forgot about it. In the past, I was sure that we would never be a couple again, so why this experience?

Within a couple of days, I received a phone call from his family telling me that he had passed away on the very day that I had this experience with him. I then realized that he finally had all of the answers about the things he didn't understand about me and life in general. I also realized that he had created the experience we shared; what he created seemed as real as any of my normal daily experiences in life. I felt that this was his way of making all the wrong in our past relationship right before he moved on. I also realized that he now knows that there is life after death, something that he didn't believe in prior to his death. I was pleased to know that the torment that he often experienced in life due to his spiritual confusion had finally been resolved for him.

After this happened, I was speaking with a friend of mine who is psychic when unexpectedly she mentioned the fact that he had passed on and that I was lucky because he always loved me very much, but he just couldn't get a grasp on life in general due to some kind of confusion in his life.

I feel that what happened with Robert in our last meeting after his death was a great cleansing for me and for his soul and karma, for lack of a better word. If he had not created this experience, he would have been carrying that baggage with him and it would hold him back, or slow him down with his spiritual evolution. He also needed this opportunity before he could go on; it was his way of making things right, something he had always tried to do in the past but was never able to follow through with. I am very grateful for this experience with him as I have always wished the best for him and continue to do so today. I know we will meet again during our spiritual evolutionary process.

## Topic # 22:  Transition from Life

My immediate family and several relatives have also had many supernatural experiences similar to mine during this incarnation on Earth. My mother was one of those people. She discussed many of them with me in before she passed on.

In her lifetime, she also experienced what it was like to be involved with several churches that were very dogmatic. She was religious more so than spiritual and concerned for my safety due to my belief in so many so-called mystical events that I had experienced in my life, even though they were always positive and uplifting spiritually and emotionally. To me, it was nothing more than the reality of life and death because I had lived it but again she sometimes was concerned based on the beliefs that the older generation had handed down to her generation.

She knew that I believed in God as the highest power. She understood and often commented that I lived a very spiritual life and was always the most caring person when it came to the needs of others. She still had some concerns that the positive spiritual events might actually be negative and someday turn against me. She eventually learned that my guidance was pure and that I would be just fine when it was time for me to leave this Earth permanently.

She also experienced several miracles in her life. I think her most important miracles were her visits with Jesus. She had a visit with Him early in her life and several visits near the time of her death. The first visit was when she asked people at her church to pray for her. She had smoked cigarettes since she was in her teens and had not been able to stop that bad habit. A short time after her prayer request, she was sitting in the living room embroidering. She looked up just as Jesus appeared in full-body form right in front of her. He reached out to her. She thought He wanted her to go with Him.

Her habit took over instead of her instincts. She looked at His outstretched arm and said, "Wait until I get my cigarettes." She reached for them on the table beside her as she got up to go with Him. He vanished right before her eyes. She felt very sad about the way it all transpired, but her cigarette habit was broken forever.

Many years later, she developed an illness that became terminal. Her doctor told her she had six months to live. She only lived about a month or so after she reached that stage of her illness. Though she was gravely ill, she still had a very sharp mind, which amazed all of us. Sometimes she was more alert than any of us, and then there were times when she appeared to be totally absent from her body. During that time period, her transition took many twists and turns.

Several times, we thought she had made her final departure, but she always came back to share with us about who she had visited with in Heaven. These visits were with Jesus and people she had known in her lifetime. She returned so many times because she was not finished with the things that she needed to clear up on Earth. She had to make all of these visits to Heaven before she was ready to allow her body to shut down completely.

When she was actually ready to make her final departure, she returned from her last visit to Heaven to finalize things with her immediate family. She came back to tell us about her latest visit with Jesus and to say goodbye to us. She was finally prepared to leave her body after this visit with Him.

She said Jesus told her that He knew who I was and that all was well with me. He also told her that He would be coming to take me when He was ready for me. This was what she needed to hear because I had not gone to church every Sunday of my life, as she had wanted me to. She wanted to be sure that all of her children would make it into Heaven when our time came. She didn't understand that we could have our own church in the back yard under a tree and it would be equally sacred. She had this way of thinking because church was a big part of her life.

Over the years, she was never radical about any of those issues. She never mentioned it to me unless I brought the subject up. I guess it was just a motherly instinct to protect her children. She knew that spiritual encounters of all sorts could take place because of her own experiences; she knew she was spiritually protected.

When I realized that she was finally ready to pass on, I verbally assured her that everything would be alright. Although she didn't appear to be alert or even conscious at the time, I felt she could hear me or that her soul would get the message. I told her that I loved her very much, that all was well with the whole family, and that she had done her job perfectly. The minute I finished talking to her, she raised her pointer finger as if it was a gesture to signal that she heard the message. After this last goodbye, she was finally able to pass on.

I was so lucky to have been able to be there for an extended stay with my mother during this last illness. Not only did I get to help take care of her but to spend personal time with her. It was important for me to help her work through all of the things she needed to clear up in order to go peacefully into Heaven.

Thankfully we had Hospice nurses and Betty, our private nurse, there to assist us with taking care of her medical needs. I am thankful they were there for her and also for my Dad when he was terminally ill. In case you don't know who Hospice is, they are a healthcare option for patients and families who are faced with a terminal illness.

## Topic # 23: Visitor from Heaven and 9-11 in New York

Several years after my mother passed on, she paid a personal visit to me in my home. It was a total surprise to me. I wasn't sure that she understood that she could communicate with me after she had gone to Heaven.

This particular visit from her occurred shortly after the major tragedy in New York on September 11, 2001. Just as I sat up in bed, she appeared right in front of me and started speaking to me telepathically. She said, "You were right about all of the things you tried to tell me regarding God and the other spiritual studies that you were into. I wish I had listened to you and learned more about all of those types of things while I was still living."

She went on to say, "I am currently stuck in a place where I have to study all of the same spiritual teachings that you tried to tell me about. I cannot move forward in Heaven until I learn all of this and have a better understanding of how spiritual evolution works. I am now anxious to move forward quickly with this process."

I then asked her if that place where she was located had a name. She replied, "I don't know the name of it; I just got here. I was transferred because so many people came in all at once. It was overcrowded so they had to move me to this new place."

I felt comforted knowing she was now aware that the spiritual and metaphysical teachings I told her about were true, since it was such a concern for her on Earth near her time of death. I later had one of those Aha! moments as I realized what she had to say that morning made perfect sense about the overcrowded situation and why she had to be relocated from her original location. This visit to me occurred right after the 9-11 event, which was why she said that there were so many people coming into Heaven all at once. She made no mention of that date or event, so I assumed that she knew that I would automatically know it was due to the 9-11 incident, but it took a while for this fact to hit me.

Her early morning visit was very important to me in many different ways. I felt good about where she was, as she sounded very happy and jovial in her conversation with me, just like her normal self. She was no longer in pain or sorrow from earthly matters. After her visit ended, I missed her but knew that she had to move forward with her own spiritual evolution and that I would see her again someday.

Mom's visit validated what I have experienced spiritually in so many different ways. It validated the fact that there is physical life in Heaven because she spoke about the lack of housing that the large group of people coming in all at once had created. It also validated that she now knew I was correct about the teachings and knowledge I had learned and tried to share with her while she was on Earth.

It was important for her to tell me and important for her to finally know I am safe according to the teachings she was now learning in Heaven. As you may recall, she had felt that she could not leave Earth until she knew that I was spiritually safe and that nothing negative would cause me harm.

## Topic # 24:  Heaven Reverts Age

Another very special visit that I had with someone who had passed on was with my grandmother. This visit was many years after she passed away. This time it was actually me paying the visit to her at her present Heavenly location, but not by my own doing or thoughts. I just ended up there without notice. It was as if I was transported into another physical realm of existence that I now understand as being another dimension.

I found myself standing just inside the doorway of a room that was filled with people. They were all dressed as if this was a semiformal occasion that I had popped in on. It looked like a modern-day social gathering. People milled around and talked in groups.

I didn't recognize anyone and wondered why I was there with all of these strangers. I turned to look at two men that stood in the middle of the room; both wore well-tailored, dark suits. As I gazed between the suited men I saw a group of ladies sitting on a sofa on the far side of the room. I spotted three women sitting on a sofa and immediately focused on one specific lady that was sitting in the middle; she appeared to be about forty-five-years old. I thought she looked familiar, but I couldn't figure out who she was. Then our eyes met, she gave me a big smile. At that point, I knew that she was my grandmother on my mother's side of the family.

I hadn't recognized her right away because she looked so much younger than I would have expected. She was in her early sixties at the time of her death. I had seen pictures of her when she was around the age of forty-five or even younger, and she looked very much like she did in those pictures. What is even more bizarre about her age is that she had passed away at least thirty years prior to me seeing her there in this social setting, which makes me wonder if people in Heaven actually age. I had not seen her earlier in Heaven, so I am not sure. After I recognized her and was greeted with a smile, I suddenly found myself back on Earth.

The entire event was different from the other visits I had experienced. As I have said before, with the kind of life I live, I never know what to expect. The fact that each event is different actually makes it more believable for me; it gives me less to argue with myself about. It also allows me to know without question that the experiences are real. This event was not only a greeting from my grandmother but to show us that a social life goes on after death.

After that visit with my grandmother, I had a visit with another family member, James. He passed away a few short years ago when he was in his sixties. As usual, I thought of him often and wondered why I had not received a visit from him. I almost wasn't expecting him to pay me a visit because I assumed that he might not understand that he could visit people on Earth after leaving here because he, like my mother, really wasn't into any of the same spiritual beliefs that I was. In recent years, we had had a few conversations about some of my spiritual beliefs and he seemed to be warming up to my understanding of how life's evolutionary cycle works, but that was about it.

This year on his birthday, I sent out a mental thought to him to say happy birthday. Within 48 hours, he appeared to me. I saw that he now looked as though he was in his twenties. He didn't stay long enough to communicate but I was grateful and thrilled to see him briefly and to see that he was alright. He obviously had the knowledge that he could create the visit, but I am guessing that it would be a practice that anyone would have to work with to develop; similar to the way the male character did in the movie Ghost.

This pattern of people looking younger after they have passed on seems to be the rule of thumb, for lack of a better word. I am happy to see this and it seems to me to be a logical way for this to happen instead of being an infant that needs care. I have never known an infant that passed away or heard of anyone seeing or visiting with an infant in Heaven but I am curious to know what that age would be like.

### Topic # 25:  A Funeral in Heaven

When my stepfather passed away, I was not feeling well enough to fly up north for his funeral, much to my regret. He didn't let that stop him from creating that experience for me. Miracles never cease in my life, thank God and my other miracle-working Angels that guide me through life.

One morning, I awoke, did my morning stretches, and then sat up to get out of bed. Before I could get out of bed, I found myself at a funeral. It was my stepfather's funeral, which had already taken place up north a few years before.

I found myself standing near the casket but never looked in it, which seemed odd to me after the fact. There were a lot of family members there standing around and talking to me. The stranger thing was that the people I talked with as I stood by the casket were people that were also not able to attend his funeral.

After spending time visiting with the other family members there, I decided to leave the building by myself. I walked down a long sidewalk that led to a huge cathedral. When I got to the end of the sidewalk, I stood looking the beautiful cathedral. It reminded me of Duke Cathedral in Durham, North Carolina—it was very ornate.

Then, I saw my stepfather standing there in front of these huge doors. He looked very young compared to the way he did when he was alive, because he was elderly at that time. He just stood there all by himself until he saw me standing on the sidewalk. He walked towards me. The next thing I noticed was how handsomely dressed he was. He was wearing a beautiful designer outfit that looked as if it had been tailored for him; everything about it was perfect. He was wearing a black suit, shiny black shoes, a white shirt, and a black-and-white patterned tie to match.

I recall saying something to him that seems strange to me now in retrospection. I was thinking that since I had not seen anyone in the casket in the other part of the building that I really wasn't sure whose funeral it was. I asked him "Why aren't you at the funeral?" He replied, "I went to this door," pointing to the large cathedral doors, "and nobody was there." I told him that he had gone to the wrong door. This building was configured in an 'L' shape with two sets of doors, one to the larger portion of the building and the other to the right of the 'L' shape. Then I told him that I would walk him over to the correct location.

I had spent a lot of time with him right before he passed and knew how frail he had gotten. My memory of his past condition caused me to put my arm around him to stabilize him as we walked. I quickly realized that he didn't need stabilizing. He was as strong and sturdy as a body builder, much to my amazement.

As we reached the correct door where the casket was located, he stopped, turned and looked at me and said, "I wanted to make sure that you were able to be at my funeral." At that moment, I vanished from his side and was back on my bed in a seated position.

It seems as though all of this was created for me so that I could be at his funeral. After his death, he obviously knew that I had wished I could be there for him. The visit that was created allowed the fulfillment of his wish as well as mine.

The very next morning after my visit with my stepfather, I awoke to another visitor from the other side. It was my Aunt Pam this time. She had passed on into spirit world, as I sometimes refer to it. Aunt Pam looked half the age that she was when she died. We were just starting to get into a conversation when my phone rang, and she vanished from my home. I was sad that I was not able to visit with her longer. Even though I have had numerous visits with friends and family during their time on the other side, it is always such a pleasure to have these experiences; it makes me wish for more, as I miss them very much.

I thought it was interesting that Aunt Pam's visit came the day after my stepfather's, as they were not blood relatives but were related through marriage. She was my mom's half-sister. I felt that it was no coincidence that both visits occurred near the same time. It was as if my family members, as a group, had focused in on me at that time and all of it had been orchestrated in the same manner that I have grown accustomed to. In my mind's eye, I can just see all of the family discussing me and then arranging their visits to me.

Each visit with family and friends has brought me more proof that life goes on after death. With all of this proof, how can I deny that fact? It seems from a lot of my experiences that when we are in Heaven, we are with the same immediate family members and at least some of the same friends that we are with on Earth during this lifetime.

Each of my heavenly visits has been unique and special in their own way, but the reality remains the same: death is not the end of life, our souls live on, and Heaven is a physical place. This isn't a belief for me at this point, but rather a matter of fact.

## Topic # 26:  Dimensional Travels and
## Learning Experiences

I never cease to be amazed with the way my guides manifest such amazing information that in the end always shows me that they truly are aware of 'all that is' in the universe.  Their information gives me confirmation in one way or another that I am on the right track with them.  Another example of their handy work is this: after I had the majority of this book written they showed me two quotes from Nikola Tesla.  Those quotes spoke to the very thing I had just written about and they are included in the early part of this book.  For me, this drove the point home more strongly than ever that the guidance of these all-knowing entities is very precise; it leads the way home.

I am very grateful for all of my life experiences and amazing dimensional travels that  have taught me so much. Additionally I am thankful to have had the honor of learning from my guides; the co-authors of this book.  Their teachings came in the form of dictations, visions, and magical manifestations, as well as their orchestration of events that have given validation to their teachings.

Through all of my fascinating adventures I found the mesmerizing dimension of Heaven to be the most meaningful and soul evolving. The lives in that realm are fully functional from what I have witnessed. The residents of Heaven seem to be living in the moment of each second or experience. Everything seems effortless and flows naturally, as if being in the moment allows life to happen in that manner with little or no effort, almost like magic; and again, things that need to get done just happen.

This heavenly lifestyle sounds like a place I would love to relocate to when I leave Earth permanently, unless of course, I achieve the highest consciousness to be able to go straight to the God-Source to reside. In the meantime, I will continue to visit these magnificent locations and share my journeys.

Here's hoping that my life's journey has given you the 'ins and out of Heaven', a clear understanding of your roadmap to Heaven and life's evolutionary cycle.  This education was intended to help you in evolve spiritually by applying the portion that rings true to you, or simply gives you the confirmation that you were looking for regarding your own beliefs.

In the beginning, I set out to discover how our cycle of life functions on Earth and throughout the universe by gazing at the stars. My curiosity as a child led me to the answers I share today; in the end I found that star-gazing really does pay off.

~   If you wish to receive notification of future revelations from these powerful guides please email us at UniversalChanges@triad.rr.com . We respect your privacy; we do not share email addresses.

www.ingramcontent.com/pod-product-compliance
Lightning Source LLC
Chambersburg PA
CBHW020517030426
42337CB00011B/428